24 YEARS OF VEX AND SLATHER

POEMS BY JEREMY L. HILL

Copyright © 2018 by Jeremy L. Hill
All rights reserved

No part of this publication may be reproduced, stored in or introduced into a retrieval system, or transmitted, in any form or by any means, without the prior written consent of both the copyright owner and publisher of this book. For information and permission to reproduce selections from this book, write to "publisher" at Hungry Skies Publishing, Las Vegas, NV, USA

www.hungryskies.com

ISBN-13: 978-1-7326332-0-9
e-book ISBN-13: 978-1-7326332-1-6

Cover design and layout: Hungry Skies Publishing

Books are available in quantity for promotional, educational or premium use.

FOREWORD

First, a word about you. Thank you for your indulgence. Genuinely and sincerely, thank you.

Now, a word about me. Some know that over the years, various, not-very-important journals and the like, have been friendly to my efforts. This is a continuation of that effort. And, to be frank, writing is about me, not you. Again, thank you for your indulgence.

Sometimes it's all a blur, ranging from dark to light with judgments rendered too quickly or not at all. I have avoided the outright biblical, but recognize that all poetry that addresses any argument, whether merely psychic, or in the living, is by definition, biblical. The weird punctuation is purposeful and for effect.

The title includes a number and that number could be considered a long time. No pain lingers on. It was simply time. I hope it is all worth something, maybe now, maybe later. Maybe only in the process. I don't know. Still, I genuinely thank you.

Jeremy L. Hill

CONTENTS

Foreword..
Green Gone Red 1
Fast Versus Now 2
It's All Wrong 3
No Longer A Kid 4
Outsider To The Outsider 5
You Wouldn't Believe This Is Me 6
A Friend of Mine 7
Rolling Our Fill 8
Paint 9
Parade 10
"Positive Spring 11
Sickly One 12
Stop The Cheetah 13
The Bridge Is Me 14
Transient 15
Absolute Control 17
Names 18
My Source 19
My Place 20
Metal Box 21

24 Years Of Vex And Slather

Lovely K 22

It Comes 23

I Need A Car 24

My Greedy Love 25

Good Tattoo 26

Generous Portion 27

Fear Of Smoke 28

Even Now 29

E, At First 30

E, Later On 31

E, Is For me 32

Rain On The East End 33

Confidence 34

Bravo Beautiful.. 35

Bees... 36

Barcelona As A Child 37

And There I Was 38

Pretty Tonight 39

The Lions Being Still 40

This Gentle Man 42

What You Want.. 43

The Priest 44

Rightly Theirs.. 45

The Hatch	46
Grandma Swam To An Island	47
Under The Bed	48
Valuable	49
He Will Help Us All	50
The Big Idea	51
Sea Heart	52
Not Alone Enough	53
Cured By Love	54
It's All Style That Brought Us Together	55
A White Pill Of Hope	56
I Am Not A Warrior	57
Sadness Of Columns	58
Why The Fright	59
Spires Down	60
Wine Of Days	61
The Separate Maze	62
Help From An Ephemeral Place	63
Mother's Sweetness Of Days	64
Grand Comparison Of Lives	65
My Type Of Courage	66
Martyrs And Fools	67
Working Every Day To Live	68

Lisa	69
Red Jacket	71
Doe Eyes	72
She Took Care	73
The Company	74
Hardhat True	75
Towers	76
Expecting Hailstones	77
Trembling Affirmations	78
The Thing I Want The Most	79
Constantly	80
Small People	81
Brushing	82
You're So Perfect	83
Captivated	84
Often Pardoned	85
Cocoon	86
Climbing A Mountain	87
Within Being Without	89
Stubborn Drawings	90
Morning Harvest Made By You	91
Those Places	92
Golden Sea Love	93

Meanwhile, Cassidy Mirror, You Are Hurting Me	94
The Philosophy of Matt	96
Chiseling Away At Myself	97
Harder Crystal Mountains	98
Pushing It All Away	100
Talking To Everyone	101
Rocky Getting Shook	102
My Blinding Early Shine	103
White Streaks On My Ceiling	104
I Miss You Big Tex	105
Waites the Torrents of Torment	106
Laughing at Art	107
Plastic Not Fake	108
The Beautiful Road	110

GREEN GONE RED

It dulls the pain for everything.
For which,
of which,
I am missing out.

Each and every time I am tame,
a part of me dies (so deep down in my spirit bones).
But I am halves.
With them I am, without, a doubt,
me as I should be, as a man, as a wounded but loved man.
He is but a warrior, tearing through the defenses the elastic ledger and shrill accounts.

To balance, it makes no sense.
It twists my insides so I poison those green leaves of each half only to wake ever more in pain for calm,
wanting that which cannot be but strictly singed and chaffed and put aside (in later years, one hopes).
Duty may decide,
but if moments are measured close,
not near,
that love has no chance,
as fear of being it all,
goes unnoticed through thickets of slightly bleeding drops and jaundiced homes known, oh so,
known.

FAST VERSUS NOW

Tie your love to the ground,
oh silliness of you – gravity,
you are nothing,
calling us,
we are there, already,
so far ahead and further coming soon which is never in this moment,
not enough.

Because fast lives live on.
Always, they do, they will, they must, or we all perish completely and then gravity has won (again).

Not right now, has it.
It has not, so long as the axial spinning is pinned to the mark of all of our corded eyes,
for one single, soft, moment.

That is all you get.

IT'S ALL WRONG

It's all wrong.
I eat more.
I care more.
I drink more.
I sleep less.
I work more.

I am poor.
I am going to sleep, diet and do nothing but play with the kids.

I hate more.
Me.
I love more.
Standing in the way, oh he is a wicked one with a curving autumn smile.
He doesn't really care for slight of hands, it is all odorless bombast.
Until he is back to me, when the blood boils the eyes from inside to out, rendering to syncopated tears.
Staring at the devolved city we built.
The crime.
The filth.
The humans, they are sometimes kind.

Not right now.
Not with me.
I am the wrong.

NO LONGER A KID

Trying to make the reflection fly,
the black cat misses his shadow in the proximate nighttime,
all the while,
the curses are slung from the balconies of unwashed hands searching for the next sweet plant in the frozen ground of souls.

A wail.
Sure of themselves and soft.
Too soft.

It is settling around,
neither moving away nor from within.
A lingerer.
Reminders that past that post,
it is,
the last time to see,
through disheveled sheets hung for the tender slumber.

And what a long slumber it is.
Damn the night. Even it moves too quickly.

Even.
A wail, too soft.

OUTSIDER TO THE OUTSIDER

So long, an outsider looking in,
maneuvered to be an insider.
Still looking in,
at the insiders,
so comfortable in their status,
and me with nothing still.

At the same time that I had everything and all,
which, I could not see or feel as it was,
still,
unrecognizable to the Me.

Waiting, I soon ran out of practicality and flow,
all the while,
My riches,
surrounded Me again, and daily again.

I was less than average but more than most, ignoring my riches, severely devoted to ghosts.

YOU WOULDN'T BELIEVE THIS IS ME

The closer I get the hotter I become,
pounding head and absent heart.

This is my fantasy death and I am walking with eyes wide open into its rock-hard pit.

I am not a pretty sight mumbling to myself,
my own words tripping in front of the stairs leading toward this open wound,
heart racing while mathematically computing the costs of extreme howling and baying,
only to measure a grey Scandinavian self.

Afterwards, I conjure that it's just another opportunity to start again, afresh and anew.
I am sorry that these conflicts are so hard,
my dear.

A FRIEND OF MINE

Awoke one morning with the pang,
it never left me.

Drugged it, clubbed it and neglected it.
Nothing.
Family history, I am told.
Not a secret this should have been.
Just relax, relax.
Right.

You don't even know, you're a goddamned rabbit,
run.

In the cage,
hiding food in one corner only to move it again.
too nervous to eat at that trough even though it was always full.

The guillotine was always somewhere nearby,
plainly hidden.

ROLLING OUR FILL

Lay there with you.
Listening, knowing you know it too.
Knowing you feel it,
its kindness of luscious waves,
rolling to you through me.

I'll even let you choose,
let's not say a word,
just listening,
with me in every grimly guided was filling us up.

The sweat, on a horse's back, being cold, from rain his rider never felt.
You're the only person I know whom I can listen with.

PAINT

A windswept world with dark and puffy caricatures,
where I am indistinguishable from the vacant, un-lasting,
ten thousand nights,
evaporating harshly like the smell of gasoline.
off of the water's edge.

I would paint this scene as through the mouth of your owl,
with oozing, slippery boats,
aware of the gasoline,
like teeth and soft tissues sharper and harder with each movement.

But, I don't paint.
Like most people, I can't seem to remove myself from the luxurious wasting.

Be gone now.
Or, paint, paint, paint.
The time is the giving canvass.

PARADE

Sitting there the papers flew all around.
A ticker tape parade just for me.
Just for me!

Undisturbed by the golden ghosts,
the lovers caught in their tempest storm,
forced to embrace to shut out their cruel surroundings,
tightening the lid on a personal tincture box.

And more papers flew by,
and I, only I,
sat there in still reverie,
in the parading street filth.

"POSITIVE SPRING

Growing newly,
blooming in multi-color plumes,
recovering from the long winter,
dirt more dirty with the wet water of this consistent spring.

It can wait.
Let it wait until the hospital bed is shaken of its last gasp.
This is the godly surgery we've been awaiting,
always a positive spring.

SICKLY ONE

Are you not my savior?

Yes, the bulging ribs, nightly pain, and bloating galore.

Saying the splendor will be cut, how can you say that?

Stripped bare, the microscope has a crystal palace of its own pain,
do not ask for the fixed outcome,
which hardly matters in the weight of ounces as it is the same weight of remorse.

It takes a lot of tears to fill up a heavy jar,
which you do not have,
and the plans are made without a known deity,
mattering not about circumstance or fate, only the circle.

Focus on the circle.

STOP THE CHEETAH

Item one on the 'to do' list,
stop the cheetah.

You say its drama… I say its cowardice.
You say you don't see it… I need you,
to slap me, hurt me, take me back
stop the cheetah.

I crushed my watch under foot,
I picked up the glass and bled my hand,
I'm wearing this mask bleak as soot,
I want to remember, but the hourglass… the sand.

THE BRIDGE IS ME

You can't have all my lives,
even though I love you so much,
neither bridle nor band,
no matter how taut or high off the water.

The build, the stature and the progress of the bridge,
bluely functioning every moot day,
passing itself off as ever standing still yet new every questionable day.
Conjecture of the aesthetics does not prove the foundation,
it will always be a cathedral to stability through all of the lives.

That much can honestly I pledge,
I will love you forever, like my past.

TRANSIENT

"They're the ones that love the most…" he said.
He lost his years ago.
Hers' that. Him, who knows what?
He's in pain. Just wants to talk. Wants someone to sympathize with.
Sympatico.

The Blood on his greyhound nose is fresh and real.
He violated his ex's new restraining order.
Did just enough time to straighten him out,
make him realize,
he's got to get away.
Get away from her.
Less temptation,
no danger.

A youngster asked him for a smoke. He gave him the whole pack.
Generics. But still.
He's looking for work, looking for housing.
He's got to share a three bedroom with two other vets in Fort Myers.
Does housing in Canada cost a lot he asks?

57 years later he's,
starting over again, being reborn.
57 years is a long time to live and not have anything.

At 57 years you should have a house, a car, a job, a family,
not blood on your greyhound nose,
desperately searching for anyone to connect with.
Anyone to love you.

He's moving through.
The 11 dollars it cost him,
to be a transient today were spent with nothingness.
Anger, retribution and reflection,
those are tomorrow.

Sometimes we're thrown into each other's laps and the differences between the haves and the nots is as clear as the blood on the old man's Greyhound nose.

ABSOLUTE CONTROL

At first a shock,
then an opening,
inch, several inches, half a foot sometimes more.

Absolute control and it comes with automatic forgiveness. The seeker got his fish delivered in salt and crusted wounds while they gathered round with concerning and crooked smiles surely not cooking the things that are meant to be eaten in the raw.

Absolutely controlled.

Nothing better.

NAMES

I knew the moment would come.
It would finally get to me and bring a time when every day becomes inconceivable.

You are a distant, disquiet,
all in your names tonight.

Our Western fears ten days out, become an unthinkable living condition,
permanent ankle chain,
a gruesome tribute built from a pile of sooty rubble.

I'm sure your children will visit this smoldering spot and say your hardened name aloud as I say your names now, ten days removed: father, mother, son, daughter.

The dullest scissors are still made to cut and they all have jagged names.

MY SOURCE

The next stage is set and unavoidable.
God sends his love from you to me and back to you again.
It is a crystallized moment, almost neutered.
The song reflecting waves off of white marble of those ancient Greek ruins,
forever is and was not enough.

I am swept, overcome.
It is still not enough.

I became sturdy on my own,
manifested in growth and working the cycle.

I am awaiting your stages, arms, open, love, salt in my eyes.

When I'm done with this I might find another.
My source helps with those decisions.

MY PLACE

I can't stand the cat's smug smile,
or, the plant's humming,
or, the water heater's hissing-pissing,
or, the smell of our garbage, piled up.

I can't stand the sick hue of this blue room.
I can't stand the circumstances of this, simple this.

I am kicked in the pants by a whisky-breath morning that is only my own doing.
And then I know I am secure, know I'm bound.
The pain knows I am real,
that I exist.

When the blood drips from my ankle chain,
it's only because I'm trying to fly,
not because it's fastened too tightly.

And the plants at my place don't quite grow,
like they,
used,
to.

METAL BOX

She is waiting,
and so am I.
In a box listening for movement,
while I'm here to comfort her.

Better she than me,
passing time,
lightheartedly.
I try to make her laugh as a consequence of her fate.

I talk to soothe her fright so the apparitions don't haunt me with their ceramic shadows.
Where is my goddamned magic key?

She is embarrassed about the whole thing,
I'm still caught in between but better than her jarring.

LOVELY K

I am rebuffed as out of course,
traveling a river that wept for many miles,
northward to southward of corners that could not be seen.

I am not there,
yet know eventually it slows to a chaotic trickle,
remote and crucial to the soul,
the soft mound it so frequently wanted.

Missing the mark,
it is better than a fallow providence.

One lost but two found,
even flowing the river that way,
away.

IT COMES

I start my pattern of wanderings, slowly.
When a day is chill and overcast,
drab with its own ghosts,
I anticipate what will inevitably come,
even if it's still green outside.
But I am ahead of that now,
frolicking and swaying,
getting it all out before I cannot.

I am waiting for the leaves to come or go.
It's still green now.

I NEED A CAR

My friend and I are both thirty years old.
He's done well,
house, car, wife, baby, steady, job.

I am still raiding the steeplechase of middling boundaries,
no dowry, mortgage or auto having had the tacky stamina
to speed past yet.

A car and a portfolio are important in this age,
at this age,
an alarm must be rousing me somewhere to new armaments and fixtures,
not just any car, not a beater.

In ten years, I wonder if my friend and I will have anything in common?

I'll own 10 when I close my eyes tonight.

MY GREEDY LOVE

A thought of your absence sends me scurrying,
stoutly to cowardice and figurative sorrows,
even when you are there,
you might be aside.

The mere thought disturbs even in your presence.
The armies of fear invade bringing one battalion after the next,
a succession dancing to that monolithic drumbeat,
of fear.

Can you fasten yourself to me?
Can you give me assurances so meaningless, so vain, they are only for me, and my greedy, greedy love?

What wretched loss of stability have you brought upon me?
Is this the fabled love of kings and queens or just my greedy, greedy love?
You have brought this urgency, this greed.

GOOD TATTOO

I got this tattoo on my forearm to remind me to be a good person,
to my wife,
to my son,
to me,
that I know the difference between right and wrong.
99 times at least.

I look at it, the contorted faces and evil surrounding good and I know good wins.
And to think, this art, this is human flesh with rules to follow
ending in unease, when the pill sticks and the dirt tastes like it does every day.

A swift bird will prey.
But not on me.
Can't wrap its beak around this bruised and bleakly painted forearm.

GENEROUS PORTION

In my reverence for her past beauty, we met again so I could get closer to my knees,
still learning.

I've heard this story so many times.
My father told me this story,
he warned me,
but, I did not listen.
My father has his own,
these grapes are all mine.

Pour me a generous portion so my youth sashays of daring and salts our ears with identities created and gifts given.
Surely she remembers youth,
my youth.

These grapes are young and foolish,
they laugh in the faces of lions.

Pour me a generous portion.

FEAR OF SMOKE

I can still smell,
even up here, where it is safe,
and,
we are safe here, even though everyone's life just ended,
few know it yet.

I smelled you even after ten days.
But not on that day.
On that day,
I tasted you,
and it meant nothing, incomprehensible and remote.
Even if in the lungs and eyes, it eluded me by being too
obscene, unreal.

All of you poor souls are lingering,
granting me visions of visions of your days as I smell you
tonight.

I wish I knew every one of you but I fear the smoke and
the winds will shift again,
maybe bringing the slow burn to an angle of natural
repose.
I wish that as you waft away from us, ever now part of me,
lungs made sturdier by your unforgotten graces.

EVEN NOW

I recognize you in the dark,
can feel every part of you,
even your thoughts,
knowing the shape of our complex future.

One moment sustains for a day, one look for a week, one taste for month.
These are red wings and hot branded hooks of a desire.

Years and days and sands flow uneven.
My mundane is wrested away compensating with your love.
Time will pass and we may grow.
Even now.
Even now.

E, AT FIRST

I had a great time drinking her whiskey and telling her the grave and edgy.
She had a great time smiling and nodding her head with recognition, implied generosity as life laid bare.

Other comers, all vulnerable but none enough for these attentions.
Then, an utter acceptance, making the jaundiced unforgettable.
Down this road is nowhere you've not been before.

The lights will eventually fade,
eventually, your shade plants will die and everything will grey,
going down is no real loss,
being inside the self may be the last thing we remember on our death beds.

Have you ever met someone you truly needed?

E, LATER ON

Nighttime doesn't let us forget,
that we were our precious little things.
In complexity, we marked a hardscrabble and puzzling exploration.
Fantasy really, just fantasy.

We could have done anything and that is the garden.
So infrequently do we truly choose what is planted.
You were my fast and brave explorer.

The thing is moved on,
the mind lingers never having harvested the abundance that comes to the table to sloppily eat again.

E, IS FOR ME

Stand by, be my watchman.
Tell me I'm a hard man,
tough,
like the temper and sinewy muscles supporting the façade of crumbling Atlantis and of this blighted and fanciful urban decay.

This is decay in front of a wall of mirrors.

Would you do that?
Of course you would.

I'll let you chose.
The parameters are yours.
I will always feel better rolling in your dirt.

RAIN ON THE EAST END

Underneath me the cars are hissing by.
I am securely standing here,
East End, a girl, and the lonely city sound of raindrops of misfortune.

Two lovers walk by, alone and impervious.
They are snakes shedding their whole skins and revealing untold tragedies,
theirs, not ours.

Rain is wishing us well on the East End,
along the river bridge,
with my girl and breakneck thoughts,
all for a moment in relative silence and peace.

A garbage barge,
two horns,
and the cars below.
Sometimes, heaven is on the rainy East End.

CONFIDENCE

Stood beside his fears and watched them calmly.
Laughed at them and made them soft cherub smiles.
A man.

Where art thou?
Are you hiding from me?

This ride's not so bad and I've seen you before,
you were so hot, so attractive and so imperial.
I saw you once stare down the gifted murderers with impunity and grace.

Your greatest gift was not to care, reassessments your bane.
Oh confidence, the beautiful rose of amber justice.

Watch out the thorn in between.
Strong, sharp and powerful, picked it up and did not care anymore for the rose made ugly by the green stain of pricked blood.
Tears soon fell down and washed that blood away making the thorn rotted and malleable.
Weak.

Oh, confidence, you were the gift.

BRAVO BEAUTIFUL

To give to you wings tonight, to feel me on your right, on your left, leave that,
that half for which we don't care.
My warm anger, consider it the heat of hate and my gift to you.

But then I'm pulled,
back again,
and,
I remember what,
I want.

Not you and certainly neither me.

BEES

Walk down Fifth at five,
see the souls dimly lit,
their own personal canvasses deeply alive for a moment.

Watch the bees go,
and render days done and evenings open, arms out as reformed ministers taking lashes with thoughts of comfort at that place deceived as a home.

The other things we all have to do.
Reference points so far away that they become brittle with every crying eye.

The bees are off to be quieted over again.
Forgetting to sting, they will die slower.

BARCELONA AS A CHILD

In Barcelona I was with three strangers,
a crazy half-white, half-black, American man,
and two beautiful English girls.

In Barcelona I danced the nights, sweet Spanish wine on my breath, pretended no evil existed in the world to the sacred family and ghost and my followers.

In those nights I was an armored saint.

We all long for glorious Barcelona nights where even the hopes of the last partisan crowd are attached to the holy nothingness.

That is a burden,
but not in Barcelona nights.

AND THERE I WAS

And there I was,
surrounded by my own vanity and the huddled, writhing,
electronic crowd veiled in crass un-meaning.

How to be so happy when the air is so thin?
Everyone but anyone to really talk to.

And there I was, missing out on all of it.
The world's pain could wait while this vanity bought extra time.
Cocooned yet bleeding from within.

And there I was,
Amongst them, talking about the most ridiculous things.
I could not escape myself.

And there I was.
The bright translucence of all of the stars,
was little comfort when we left that wretched place.

PRETTY TONIGHT

New York was pretty tonight,
the shimmer of skyline,
ask of tomorrow still far away.

Sometimes she's just there,
devoid of light,
absent of faith,
recoiling at her own reflection.

But then all is recalled,
back to that shore where the lights cannot be avoided,
and the drunk and his misfit morning and a man in his car
driving too early to the city.

The night hides her in his folds,
his body for the skyline,
absurd with color and lives of common remorse.
Look at her now,
pretty tonight.

THE LIONS BEING STILL

And yet again the days come in this too-early fall when I think of my tragic brave-glorious friends again.

Oh, how sad I am and how I miss you,
you lions, steely strong, towering apparitions.
Why can't you be back here tomorrow?
And why do you care to represent our freedom,
never as good in your disappearing shadows,
littering the bone yard fragments,
wishing to hear your calming voices again.

Oh, I am so sad today as we turn to a vanished place lifting our veils on chases and small contrition once again seeing you so clearly.

It is not tolerable now except on this yearly occasion and in wretched, breaking seconds of weakness which we stash quickly on to damnable excuses and deadly distractions.

But today, I see your face clearer than the tides that are chained to that date.
As I see you walking towards me out of that chrome hell, I kiss you everywhere and speak loudly to you, no matter what casual observers may care.

I give you a pin sized place to rest in my heart and pull the gentle strings to prick that area. Today, I will invite you back to inhabit a much larger part of my tepid and unforgiving heart.

And today, behold, with the pulling of the string the torrent begins anew flashing with adrenal panics and thrusting with nauseating remorse.
With the day and prick again,
no man is dry and not undone.
We look up to see only a void and crisis reflects back upon us and shocks us by maintaining its strength even in the face of our ignoble pleas and faulty white liniment.

I am so sorry my friend.
I'm so sad for us and this world has lost a human momentum of faith and charity.
But I will long for you and your love this short year and see you these early fall days again.
You are but a spot now but always the size of the sun on this day,
my pride that is always still.

THIS GENTLE MAN

Bearing your unknowns,
My unsafe hear chances the run.

Don't let this gentle man lay too long with crystals,
chewing and crunching them,
with so little sound.

Intertwined by our survival now,
the crescent void is merely the timing of the ripping,
where it cannot be supplanted with your cuts of godly gentle pain.

WHAT YOU WANT

The timid don't know what it's like at that hour,
when the souls light up a tiring optionality,
of far tonics otherwise sloping away,
from the backs where heavy white wings used to stretch,
through the crater of harrowing spears,
getting us home again.

A sweet fall,
here and there,
does no one (who can keep it together) any harm.
Even the late, late ones know it's better to suffer sweetly,
with the sweat of the heat, rather than of the effort.

Don't be anything other than a doll, dear.
Don't.
It's just another part of this place and its cinnamon apparitions which can haunt all night and then again even after having been sworn off as the bloodying yoke of the end.

There is no end.

All smell of the come and go, even if hidden.

THE PRIEST

Must I know right now where this deceit creeps from,
which corner, what nasty man with his cigarette breath
and whisky smiles brings himself to me?

The sum between my teeth now,
laughing at their plight searching for that priest's hidden
grave.

You betray me tonight,
when I'm kissing you.

RIGHTLY THEIRS

Everyone being afraid of missing something,
swimming around with a beak full of peat and sand.

All woke early and in a purple spell,
couldn't shake their shaking.
And with a worsening sky, just ate and drank the sugar that was rightly theirs.

It is such hard work.
It is sometimes, when the nurse of your bastard rings again, worth it all.

A tough position to take

THE HATCH

Perfect would not do.
Invincible, will eventually tire.
The good, sweet, sunlight, goes to bed.

The hissing and deflating, carried upon the back of these storied men.

It is truly the distractions,
swapping one moment for imagination all day long,
living beyond means, in a fluff of contrivances.

Only for this simple moment,
do not stop the imagination.

Thank god that such a simple hatch is still open.

GRANDMA SWAM TO AN ISLAND

Grandma was a swimmer and she taught us to swim.
She swam the backstroke when shown the whip,
the doggy paddle when she was tired from labor and toil.

She swam to that lonely island,
where predators lurk beyond,
and strength recedes with each wave frothing like a sickly and rabid dog,
the dogs they send after each of us (eventually).

There have been consequences.

When do I feel strange?
When I am standing still on my fortified island,
each way is up with familiar kin.

When do I feel good?
When I'm on my lonely island
with solitude as a reprise,
with solitude as my prison
swimming away from you because my Grandma taught us how.

UNDER THE BED

Later, when I woke, it was under my crumpled bed,
down under, inside and below me.

Founded wings over time,
died in their own melancholy spore-dust,
crusting and rusted,
even though cleaned after use.

Regretful I'll be for the rest of my life,
no turning back to my normal,
precious and little circle on fire now.

The cannons killed us all slowly,
all of us men of mortal wings,
no matter how saintly,
there was no emaciated winner.

VALUABLE

"Douglas, I'm sure she was right," she said.
She's a liar,
a goddamned liar.
Always has been difficult like that.
They're like that,
damn shame.

The friends aren't any better,
they scheme,
 "You know?"

I could trust her,
she made my dinner,
changed my sheets,
kissed it better,
and believed in me.

I don't see any way to get that back,
It was broken in so many crafty ways.

She was wrong,
and it's a damn shame to lose such a profit center.

HE WILL HELP US ALL

I carry it in a faraway bag that brings my heaven head close when morning is dewed with obtrusive vignettes and candles that burned a sweet and recognizable scent.

It is that moment,
in the knowing.
At that moment,
I submit.
Fallen and singed and no longer caring.

I submit that this isn't so bad.
It's all temporary and laudable.
Maybe he will reward my burdens,
and a cool water will splash right into my eye,
no matter that it is closed to his crucible of lightness.

THE BIG IDEA

He slams the door on me,
face blue with drunkenness,
belly bloated with hunger,
not for food.

I tried to go for it,
but when I gave it gas,
I had to run away with the idea, which is probably what I want.

Put the pedal down slowly,
it never works well that way.

It makes me sick that I'm not totally adverse to the idea.

SEA HEART

I wish I was hearing it from the sea,
crashing against and soothing my challenge.

The babble is only a barge,
a garbage barge at that,
tricking my fatal ears,
which yearn for dusty toes and hot feet,
and eyes of willow swaying lazily at his beach.

But alas,
Gotham overwhelms,
and I am a rich man, just, as such.

NOT ALONE ENOUGH

I traveled today to get where it is quiet,
at the end of a dilapidated grey birch wood pier,
peering into the fish and swallowing a lake.

I feel like I'm fourteen again,
tagging along as a worthless interloper,
with a freckled, generic and common face.

Now I'm within reach of what I'm supposed to be reaching for.
Like a peasant without a fence, I'm part of the fiefdom of wanton and reckless.

Here I am,
resting and holding the fresh air that wasn't meant for me,
seeking out lovely stars only half visible from medicines curing all our families.

I can never get alone enough, not me
Neither can the pointless Ulysses bounding up the waters' edge.

I still hear the music from you all, my largest family,
but it is playing more slowly now.

CURED BY LOVE

The characters take their place.

A rainy night,
in an isolated apartment,
personally forecasting philosophers and violence,
out of a pulpy fodder for an open mind.

One of his characters in black and white,
drawn by humanity to step the hot crates,
he is unmasked,
by tilted,
bent,
purpose.

The darkness is hard while solitary protagonists meander,
unbelieving, but still, with love.
Just like that film I saw.

IT'S ALL STYLE THAT BROUGHT US TOGETHER

He's with his chick,
wearing his baggy pants and gold,
a Mount Rushmore display,
his is bigger.

And them.
The gang with the mod silver rimmed fly glasses, suede sneakers, and those rings.

Babes only eating what mother knows is best,
milk dripping down the face, into a savvy loafer.
Their spoons are hidden now,
so others won't become jealous.

Don't forget what brought us all together.
It laughed,
a chuckle,
bet it all.

A WHITE PILL OF HOPE

Chopped at her with an axe,
but that was way after the other stuff.

Back here,
it's a mule's weight of heft,
my world being off of me,
while she's beat and cut,
that flat edge of the knife,
a siren for her love.

It's salty but tasty,
and it will continue, ad nausea, tomorrow, again, tomorrow, forever.

I know I've been here before.
One other time,
I know it like the simple-ness of the thawing breath.

I AM NOT A WARRIOR

Less than a mile away,
still making me wait,
the powers be damned in their ascendant prerogative.

The farther I got, the more it grew.

For the warriors that surround me, I am not one of them.

I creep into my mind, looking for my best friend's revenge plate.
But still too young, I am clinging to this verge.
The insufferable, muted verge, that is as round as the fattest oak groaning in the wind and heard by the warriors but not me.

SADNESS OF COLUMNS

This is not yet a time of reflection or pondering.
That will come later.

When after battles are fought Indians will dance on their
graves with sweet fruit of their mother's heart in hand,
swaying from Eden to our garden,
a reminder of what is great was grey,
always lurking to make them all bittersweet days,
even later in their infinite reflections.

WHY THE FRIGHT

The fragrant out-of-water hull of an old rusted steamer,
covered in the pock marks of hateful and clingy clams,
it is David for one day,
until the confounding sinews whisper "never had it, never will, done deal, genes boy"
diffuse and only heard by the white birds,
whispering on the white shoulder of wicked truth.

Based on one measurement,
your fortress measurement in the wilderness of logic and cunning,
wicked truth lied to me again.

SPIRES DOWN

Four walls and a breathing heart.
Stealing what was once gold.
There sat elliptical globes with,
doll faces and weeping land.

Rings of smoke, billowing clouds.
Mother's way to cleanse and groom.

Lighted rails that support our timid truces,
she triumphs by disaster, a cataclysmic retort.

WINE OF DAYS

Wait for the night to come and take away the careless of our ordinary.

The bleak shall be driven to releasing their careless bereavement,
their hope aligning our vacant shapes through filtering and shaking pasts.

Wait for the night to take away the ordinary.
There will be mirrors to ponder our kingdom's angles.

We shall stab the steeple deep into our hearts,
once the witching trestle renders the night,
once the darkness throttles our remotest harvest.

THE SEPARATE MAZE

Lurking ahead in looming grandeur,
the peaks beckoning us with their ironic sorrows,
affecting us with unforeseen currents,
thrusting us beyond their tantalizing limits.

One pass is for courage but twice is for death.

Feels as alone as being a Sunday god,
always forgiving the overheard and the yonder peaks
always an anathema to jubilantly beating machine.

HELP FROM AN EPHEMERAL PLACE

The notes pour in,
the masters speak uneasily,
looking out the window at the small space between the two skyscrapers,
where intermittent patches of clear blue show themselves when the rest remains all muddled.

The clouds keep rolling like a lost tongue,
softly speaking between buildings where you can see the clouds,
hear anyone,
anything.

It's always clear, no matter,
as long as,
you are,
looking.

She doesn't understand that you might understand.
You might,
help,
me,
tonight.

MOTHER'S SWEETNESS OF DAYS

These are perfect days,
when that which was in between,
rock-solid and mealy,
is released gentle and sweetness.

He couldn't be kinder, with a smile for the ages,
his age,
and a taste not just of what is harvested,
but of something ever more sweeter.
Of a perfectly clear and translucent flow,
no embers,
no gates,
no filtration needed.

Nothing,
when she is so gone to us all,
nothing to protect against,
these days,
harvest them with reverence,
and great pride,
in the goods of her,
sweet labor.

GRAND COMPARISON OF LIVES

He, with the astounding consistency and,
genial disposition,
white picket and all.

Me, even these years later, spasmodic, impulsive, ashamed, happy.
Nothing but these experiences,
having lived high,
of the white paisley fiction and feats.

Those grand misses of mine,
the crumbling mornings and saline sunrises.
Thank god for that!
Thank him for the greasy hobgoblins I avoided to the ends of redolent guile.

It is now,
with these hard-lined years and their inference of (mere) hurt.
It is now,
when the older siphons wonder when leaking,
what remains between,
the seldom starboard views and their ideals,
even accounting for the feats.

MY TYPE OF COURAGE

Every single waking day,
an astoundingly simple burden to bring home,
for the entire shell to be made so adamant.

The resourceful forbearer had no monarchic mission,
unless provoked to know that the vivid snapping comes from common eminence.

Even the luminous markings are not much,
evident in tactile treatment by the mothers and fathers,
hastily turning into the sluggish saw with snippets of jittery fingernails,
waiting for the carnage of the bland edict,
never tilting heads so as to keep their incandescent tears for their own carnivorous grit.

MARTYRS AND FOOLS

The fools and martyrs all got mixed up,
and a smile came across,
where the diameter of quick and transient thinking,
along a very narrow and winding trail,
not larger than the entirety of the asking
ran straight to the ground.

Evoking musty images,
she pushed them out with locution and style,
only sweating when they grew to have that familial attitude.

Then the fight started with the foolish martyrs jumping quickly,
the catwalks shaking from their appointment to the fates.

It was tempting, but the martyrs knew all along,
only history will tempt to back the righting of the scales
so that the fools can no longer besiege the blasphemous truths.

WORKING EVERY DAY TO LIVE

When the drip fills up,
it's usually morning time,
with its yellow and bloated hope,
merging forget and forgive,
as they pool in rocky eddies,
looking for excuses to jump into Sunday shadows,
so they can hide their faces from themselves.

And the wires which extend rigidly,
across chasms,
they are tight,
pulled by whom?

And how hard to fly across?

Not that much.
But flight so long ago,
was to a well-lit apartment,
with the comfort of home,
not yours' which allowed you to dream in false remittance
of the soul.

Now go forth,
as we all do,
through the curved fall of the shade,
simple, sweet, reminders of,
how far we traveled,
foot after measly foot on that wire.

LISA

I go back to home,
to where it first happened for me,
and it might be thirty years ago,
but I can remember a damn sure lot of it,
a giraffe's neck of excitement in those memories.

Oh Lisa,
it's like our lives just passed before us,
you with your untimely, murderous absence,
me with my meandering changes,
both always sharing in the symphony's greedy discovery.

I go back home,
home being the place on earth where I will return to the famished worms,
no matter the other glorious locales still claiming crumbs and the whiter specks in my teeth,
I see you, Lisa.

Home, when I am driven past that old jalopy Holiday Inn,
where your mother so liberally gave you the true compass and goods of adulthood,
I will always think of you.

How does a simple farm girl become so lovely?
And to think, on that highway night I didn't stay for more (and more and again).

It must confound, but show I was only a foolish boy.
A boy, and then Lisa.

Oh Lisa home, you are tragically gone,
and the time sticks to the sluice in my molded containment.
I vaguely know to be outraged,
yet tired of forlorn grinding.

I will think of that moment,
our trek,
its roots so long as mine beats with the clarity of home,
every once in a while.

RED JACKET

That red jacket saw a lot,
by crushing the confusion and littered angst,
protecting me from rickety and shorn table legs.

All across the smudges and stains and years,
her zipper still works,
creaky and slow, but cutting,
navel out and freed of droplets,
pale when reflecting in primrose strength.

Maybe the red jacket got tired.
She seemed to turn pedestrian,
still worn proudly, accented logos and all,
protecting the desert inside, dry and crystalline,
from the business of heat and suffering,
wrought out there.

No wonder I wear that damn red jacket.
Incessantly, with an x-ray on my heart.

DOE EYES

You all already made it,
I still have doe eyes.
You're exhausting your jazzy sounds,
and frying pan successes.
I still have doe eyes.

Handle my leaning-head and,
lean further so as to drift the places as,
I can't seem to get out of my garage,
a rather dark and sultry place,

They well up, but the tiredness,
of blank spaces and deleted times,
dilates in substantially planned ways.

You all, over there, jazzy, breezy,
still looking,
through my doe eyes.

SHE TOOK CARE

She took care of this wondering man,
sewing bronzed tenderness,
allowing brittle seeds to be planted,
often stopping the graceless and bright exams,
pulling the rowdy briers,
to remove the flicker of our ungoverned and contemplative states,
and to reassure our luxurious hope.

THE COMPANY

Dine well tonight my friend,
after all, all men are friends when it comes right down to it,
being a good friend to myself,
taking more and more of myself, for thyself, tonight.

Soon every creature comfort will become handsome and exorbitantly efficient,
a bee before his death,
still buzzing even though the honey has been all made.

Sweet dreams good friends,
let us celebrate the imperial days of cobblestone feasts and wanton purple violence,
now we eat at the trough of hardened steel and coded neurosis,
nothing like the company we used to keep.

HARDHAT TRUE

Hardhat walks by,
with casual disregard for the weight,
on his Roman shoulders,
unlike the weight beating a triumvirate hole,
in him again and again.

He asks, why does he do it?
What's wrong with him?
We only see that Styrofoam heaviness and not,
the mangled little bird fluttering in him,
waiting,
for his special sword to bare down in him,
a sonorous humanoid,
bulging, this time again, in the insides,
pushing, getting pushed (in),
submitting to the instinct of the stolen mind.

TOWERS

Imagine the bare heart against the unending and shimmering window,
naked, bloodied, confused,
ticking so hard it forgot it was a heart.

And I,
and it,
scraped ourselves away,
eyes laden with decomposed stories of towering tongues and raspy intrigues.

The premise of being such a tower,
never to be heard,
being so near and hot.

Obviously, she tricked me.
Loin cloth falling as the bodies run away.
Obviously, the vile poison corrupts faster than we all could run,
or fall.

EXPECTING HAILSTONES

She sends the S.O.S. screeching,
morning, every damn morning,
after the plausible rabbit method is rejected and the hard and clear bushing machine is sat on the glass table with gloved and saucy hands,
it comes down to what kind of umbrella to take (again) with me.

I'm constantly expecting hailstones.
Really goddamned big ones with rumpled divots and rotten cores.

One day she'll send down sweet cherries instead and I'll tip my umbrella upwards to catch them in the blasting air.

TREMBLING AFFIRMATIONS

Breathes in the moisture,
forget that poultice, dried air out there,
this is me again.

Absent mortal flattery,
it is the cutest of chirping,
just the lightness of them,
these winners of my graceless and trembling affirmations.

Reaching back with daisy eyes,
I am no longer straight,
I am cursive stripped from the letters,
never changed, here not a phantom,
hidebound, subject to all of Saint Vincent's volcanic laws,
giving my communion to them without any pain.

This is me again.

THE THING I WANT THE MOST

The thing I want the most is the thing I can't find (the most),
And when I find it,
I will hardly want it,
Until it leaves me,
behind,
desiring it again until I lose it with thoughts of finding it,
again,
in a better way,
neck, body, torso.

And friends are the fickle ring of society,
with its frighteningly sweaty temper so obsessed with midnight tongues.

CONSTANTLY

Searching for her anonymous scent,
forced me to kiss the red Christian tattoos,
while her chaste and pilgrim ghost is trapped in hell,
forced to lie between a resistance and lips of the host.

Constantly seeking is cutting me deeply.

There are trade-offs,
full-speed is what I do.

The running is at full strength,
with the only other possible destination,
fools,
surrounded in their purifying mud,
constantly, rusting with each stony bickering.

SMALL PEOPLE

The man told me "the bravest thing you can do is cry."
That was a lie.
It hurt because I thought it through, to the very end.

At the end of the sacred bond,
were only my own reflective brown eyes,
and another hot amber tear patterned on the last one's streaking sickness.

Ants carry eight times their weight,
but we only have two legs for these burdens you
leave us with,
and,
some growth is stunted forever,
no matter the size of the man.

BRUSHING

Don't think bad thoughts this morning.
That tree, it will be there in 100 years.
Some legacies are oaken,
some are not even when measuring for brightness.

Brush past the doubt made certain by fear.
Look at the wind blowing this renewed green love.
Care not for the hurt that bends knee and flexes the unbalanced tendons.
Focus on the child,
this will remain.

Take comfort as some legacies are oaken,
some are not.

YOU'RE SO PERFECT

No matter how perfect,
the truth I learned after years of us was newborn and captured.

Truth be told, I'd rather just settle my accounts, call in the fibs and lies.

After all, it was me I was lying to,
and,
I,
 was looking for someone,
 you,
could never be.

That doesn't account for the heirlooms passed around as hot rocks,
jawbreakers in a jar of your clustered things,
some convinced,
were part of the bailing hieroglyphic mountains,
placed before us for tripping the years.

I saw that design in its particular form and recognized the perfect approach.

CAPTIVATED

And if you follow me there,
we will show you the tree,
the tree of kings and queens,
I promise the tree never dies,
it's our secret, you and I.

Captivated, yet trained to be wary,
when looking up at hideous rays of hope,
riding on merciful steeds,
knowing of the good that comes from our collective deeds.

I wanted to do everything,
but you can't do everything,
so it all passed me by,
because when you choose it's just another way to deny.

I'm walking down this rusted out track where the dandelions and crosses never miss their unfastened marks, captivating the goodbyes.

OFTEN PARDONED

This is the opportunity of a lifetime.
Put down the near misses vague enough to make sides hurt and flush in recycled wisdom.

Miss the joy and deal in the suffering,
the home remedies no longer work,
and,
in the evasion of formalities,
 we so often pardoned results with crusty dilution kept in the back of our minds.

Now strike at us with vicious bitterness as we swallow our pills,
we know you don't condone this clubby slate we have put forth,
we know the gauze pad you're commuting is severely yellowed,
of our caustic vices.

COCOON

Butterfly always has her cocoon,
hanging to it as the morning hangs to the night,
no matter how far she goes.

She sees a different light,
a different color,
never bright enough or burning with enough intensity to
chill the heart of her still beating cocoon.

It's far away and she's buffered by unearthly winds.
It's a chill that has only one soluble compromise.
There will only and always be one way to warm.
It is a gift and nothing more.

CLIMBING A MOUNTAIN

Searched east and west,
and then settled on a mountain to climb,
a tall and gracious mountain more pleasing than I had ever seen,
begging me to come forward,
climb and climb.

The climbing was difficult,
a lack of reach and many rough spots made peaking a terrible fight,
but I climbed so far that one day,
I saw the top of the mountain and knew that it was in my reach.

With steepness and horrible turns,
footing became loose while rope that was still fastened below frayed in clusters giving way,
quickly away.

As I was falling,
I fell faster,
occasionally grabbing a hanging branch or sandy, washed, outcropping.

Those were not as stable as the mountain.

The mountain,

still there,
will one day,
allow me to climb without hope or fear of gracelessly falling.

WITHIN BEING WITHOUT

The belief has no speed limit,
becoming habitual until an unsuspected harbor wind,
blows sand on the wheels,
of goodly grease,
having those unlucky sands so slowly grinding,
to a place lasting of one more remote and glassy morsel.

While it was pondered daily in bankrupt hearts of terrifying retribution,
while the highway thoughts keep to themselves,
not one sign out there mattered.

STUBBORN DRAWINGS

Thank you,
for this piece of false real estate so close to embers and hearth,
it is decorated so poorly and it is exceedingly dirty,
affording me all of you,
drawn with so many red lines and broken dashes,
all carved smack down the middle of my caressing forehead.

Goddamned bastard of conviction and honesty,
thank you for your terrific help,
in laying me out,
in this glorious, sentimental fashion.

Gone but still seeping towards,
the grounded earth,
and them that are the salt,
with one more corpulent delay.

MORNING HARVEST MADE BY YOU

The throngs, the crush,
cacophonous nothing except for slipshod memories,
they harvest nothing this morning.

They are commercial phantoms mixing with the particles everyone imagined,
pushing past us,
fleeting little freedoms,
pushing past us,
gone quickly again.

Strictly speaking,
an injury here is tempered by the bouncing vibes that are weightless
and owned only by you and you alone.

THOSE PLACES

They are gone and the coup has won its violent, stoned heart,
rendering an impression of moving in unison,
succumbing ever more to the Baltic times and fates.

Everyone knows wicker rots in the Monsoon and sunny days.
It's adhering to a cellular level,
with its saliva and entrails begging for their normal place on the bone.
Any bone.

The defeat is in the unknowing,
where the senses continue to emit while the fallen,
they march,
after him,
calling his sour name while flailing,
in the time before hitting the ground.

So little is determined when the patchwork is trampled,
by sunshine legacy and furious compromises.

GOLDEN SEA LOVE

As the son almost sleeps,
her majestic concrete spires and flaring lights can still be seen,
through the crack in the window letting in the salted colors,
way at the top.

Through this window,
a little man rests and a big man hurtles himself into madness and the harm of his frictionless shine.

It's only a crack,
barely even a ticket.

Some nights it's better to close the blinds and feel the heavy breathing.
Some nights it's better to have those frail and greasy slats closed tightly,
no matter how uneven the silent cumbersome and remorseless shine.

It's such a lovely view.
No wonder we all thought of only more.

MEANWHILE, CASSIDY MIRROR, YOU ARE HURTING ME

No one is talking to me as the bleating beats,
Cassidy-ins around twin buckled Denver,
look once more to secure more wolves,
hardened to the floors.

Meanwhile, I'm on fire for you to be my bloodied ear,
guided to the heavily dented pillow,
my slick poisons surely following the reloaded trail.

Still no talking,
even knowing,
you're that one ovum always hidebound in this (of me)
quivering sight.

All these earthy and ruinously catchy things the disciplines talk to.
Try me,
so glumly and stupidly accept.

Meanwhile, the heartache,
as the grains get silkiest,
as the beats patter through the pentagon jargon fewer of us can hear.

That's the hoary and reflected push of the defaulting mirror,
from me to (maybe hopefully) you,
always a single lifeless hurt,
until the beats loudly and mindlessly finesse a crooked and grinning crack.

Until, (I have) the burning courage,
to throw away my glowing embers,
using only bare hands,
my grave silence festers,
seen only as my greedy jester.

You, all of you,
you know nothing of the art of the holy beat.
Be gone,
and let me be importantly lonely,
yelling curses at waves hitting neither shore nor surf,
betwixt the only real covenant we have with our internal beats.

THE PHILOSOPHY OF MATT

Passionate enough about our friendship to ask you the fleshy questions of bearish philosophy.

It's so urgent that we fight this battle together,
if only, this little one,
charting all directions,
except those linear smiles so gracefully embedded in our first lives.

Be with me here.
Be beyond me,
helping me outrun the far away,
semi-circle of titular thought.

Be in the real with me now,
as we take these horrendous body blows and curse the six fingered chopping blocks too slow in hewing the complication of an uncommon mother, heavy of shaking hand, seeking reminiscences aloud in spotlights hotter than every single one of their eagle stares.

Oh my friend,
Help me with this philosophy,
It is not mine, never yours, and always ours.

CHISELING AWAY AT MYSELF

With her dulcet uncolored eyes,
maybe staring back at me seductively behind her,
I'm upon her with the immensity of my felt-tipped mind,
crushing those boulders into the pebbles of our uncaring night,
so soon to be my clausterphobic craft,
me chiseling away at myself,
while harboring and then gently massaging those pebbles,
until they are so slick and smooth,
knowing each olive and sweaty groove of my cold turkey hands.

She's my boulder, my rock, no my well grooved pebble.

HARDER CRYSTAL MOUNTAINS

I haven't slept soundly for months,
the haste at which my reptile turns to cataclysmic mode is truly astounding,
wretchedly even for the ballsy cats baying in their Eastern and well-manner trees,
stretching high up and fearing the happy and natural laugh of their well-trodden enemies,
almost a chuckle, barely audible during the intermittent deluges.

I found that's not me.
They don't hear me anymore,
and I don't seek them anymore,
and I am no longer enamored with their pruned gardens,
and no longer fearful of their nightime wine cup of dismissing ire.

I don't sleep, so crystalized and so beating.
I've got these things evacuating the tracks at the slightest sulfur whiff,
prowling, deeper, dancing with a darker shadow,
following the gnarly steps,
boom, beat, step, bam, step, 123, step, again, step further,
step out to that beat,
dance with another,

an electrified drop of water hopping in the burning grease of the hotter pan.

Hotter than they ever were,
hotter on the mountain.

PUSHING IT ALL AWAY

He sat on the G train,
going downtown,
blowing his fragrant nose profusely,
eating his bloated bologna sandwich,
and mixing up, all of him,
with the paper bag drink of fame,
in plain sight that each painful gulp caused another robust blow,
pushing us all away,
after each gilded sip,
separating himself from the crass and questioning crowds calling,
the right hand,
leaving the rest of us under our breathes to unbundle him,
as another unfortunate scene,
floating on our communal sea,
surfing downtown with him pushing it all away.

TALKING TO EVERYONE

Because I'm lonely, having no real friends, having to talk to strangers.
I smile at people who could be murderers and devastatingly love what I hate and vice versa.

When you see me yucking it up with the taxi driver, the security guard, repairman, and all the little people who have no interest in selling those heavenly things that are never theirs to begin with,
it is my hallmark of camel breath desperation,
oh, at that moment, I am rash yet voluptuously building a tower so high,
no one can climb the knobby and greasy ramparts with me.

I take comfort in these row house smiles,
sharing the universal chit and chat of bins full of our own authentic cuisines,
devoid of the tastes and spices,
even the redder flash in the blacker night may cause a pang,
"where is my repairing stranger now?"

ROCKY GETTING SHOOK

Happened at that paisley building,
leaning on the ancient groove of reticent histories,
being undone by the syncopated, old school beats,
pushing the local-born losers to seek refuge,
in a paler rocking knowing no white curfews,
crust time for their bejeweled eyes,
the stacks only the minister knows.

The congregation knows.
What could be a better fruit than the 'blood red orange'
hanging subterfuge, pulpy as all hell?

True to name the sugar continues to be sweet enough,
slowly eating away the mouths,
shaping the essence with each speck,
forming the lines of crosses,
eroding the cuticles until the trembling fingers are cut to the bone.

MY BLINDING EARLY SHINE

I've seen that look before,
but it's years ahead,
can't be here yet,
the delicate gold, still flaked and falling,
still not (yet) in boxes for you to carry away,
for you to be carried, Valhalla or near.

So soon they will all be in your sun,
more sun than anyone has ever seen,
for the grace and the days that you will allow,
flying the flag of our painful want,
that the beauty near or far,
I will always know pounding the triangle butterfly wings.

Matters not that the berry may fall,
only that it was red and ripe and in the reflecting sun,
where she blinded on early days,
without knowing her own herculean shine.

I've been so early to see that look of flummoxing beauty,
and so grateful to be blinded by it.

WHITE STREAKS ON MY CEILING

Two streaks on my ceiling awaiting their elemental fixing, rumbling into all of my paisley nights with booted fairies and fumbled histories.

Don't take this good situation for the cumbersome lake where I constantly drown in your fingers.
Good advice, except for the obvious red bell that cracks from inside out when it chimes loudly to leave only the dotted condensation of the mirrors of our hot breaths.

And no one climbs the latter to fix those white streaks,
now grooved with by their uneven strokes,
getting dimmer by day and brighter by my night.

I MISS YOU BIG TEX

Man, I miss you Big Tex,
with your sweetness and leaving sincerity,
and hope with its parroting post at the gates you so badly wanted me to enter,
with my dirty clothes in your brown suitcase and sleepy vented couch,
wanting nothing to do but declare,
we are here,
we lay here,
please do let me know,
every, ever, and now again,
I know you will be Big Tex.

But you left after my joker smile crept up on you,
one finest day known from the others,
by her bloodies and oyster touring,
and button saying "now,"
but really, quite really, just "help me."

Ah damn you, sweet Big Tex,
we won't ever talk like that to each other again,
sung voices so loudly that they creak from moan to pitch,
speakers harmonious in their distortion and chorus petals,
now wailing every so often in the white canvas remorse of past years,
slipped without ever growing the mineral laden pains of each day.

I know you will be Big Tex.

WAITES THE TORRENTS OF TORMENT

Should have lived more cleanly,
not like Tom Waites, or worse,
but stuff was seen and things done,
ice cream men eventually melt all away.

It'll kill ya' after a while,
and you can trade in and out of styles for a while,
but that always ends with a case of chapped lips,
only to be cured by a good dosing of four-ten buck.

It's called voluntary self-destruction,
when the holiday season has more joy,
your head only screwed on by tomorrow's sorrows,
and the wheelchair rises and all your friends haggle in advance of the sheltering wind.

Well, bury me in the thinnest teak coffin,
with all of my stolen wallets,
the slight smile for making the hardest deadline.

Mine.

LAUGHING AT ART

We made fun of the art,
laughing at their circular seriousness,
those damn airport whiskey bandits and their never ending,
ever guarded hedges.

"You talkin' ta me?"
Well, I'm counting my change and watching my back while your bitchiness consumes us all,
thrusting at us with those overlord hips.

We wanted to see you from our dense garages and goggled houses,
where we sat comfortable in our similar pools of delta blue waters,
each playing in our one-man bands,
crooning the verses in harmony,
watching the lunatic throw rocks at his fridge and call it art.

PLASTIC NOT FAKE

Every time the candle was lit,
it looked real,
like a flame,
burning sideways and winded on its own melodies,
searching for fibrous materials more flammable,
than what was cooked into its blackest wicker hat.

Just waiting for seasons to change the souls to tread thinner than the memories.

But it gets lit again,
worse moments,
at the celebration of free flesh,
when the shrink breaks for another smoke,
banging his fist harder against the upheld and shaky hand.

When can this be fixed?
Put to a bed so warm,
the lit candle finally feels soft on each side,
the animals, all, forever,
uncontrollable in their ridiculous asphalt cages,
doors wide open and made of tinder bars,
his smoke working harder with each salty, dropping,
of the furrowed brow.

Working harder than it ever has.

Damn, that's a weak fireman.
Damn, that's a gloriously strong light.

All the while, the hyenas putting their tongues on it,
teasing, never extinguishing,
even in the sleeping trenches,
so far away, lit.

THE BEAUTIFUL ROAD

When one shoulder has already explored the other,
rubbing innocently at first,
and then with a horrid acquaintance,
deeper than the icy self-preservation,
the road becomes a mere thing,
an indeterminate distance measured in breathes,
taken in shallow gutter ditches,
mowed years past the jack rabbit sign posts.

And off they go,
humping only their sandwich breads and stolen cigs,
blistering their tongues,
making their words teeter in canyons of older voices.

They care not, not at all.

It's about peering through,
the drapes no matter,
nothing ever stopping the craven,
injustices of their spinning beings,
ever homeward,
ever wandering,
ever with gated agitations.

This limited edition book has been published by Hungry Skies Publishing. Hungry Skies Publishing is micro-publisher specializing in modern and abstract works including illustrated books, art and poetry.

www.hungryskies.com/about/

www.ingramcontent.com/pod-product-compliance
Lightning Source LLC
LaVergne TN
LVHW051504070426
835507LV00022B/2920